Lerner SPORTS

SPORTS ALL-STARS

MOOKIE BETTS

Jon M. Fishman

Lerner Publications ◆ Minneapolis

Lerner Publications Company
An imprint of Lerner Publishing Group, Inc.
241 First Avenue North
Minneapolis, MN 55401 USA

For reading levels and more information, look up this title at www.lernerbooks.com.

Main body text set in Albany Std 22.
Typeface provided by Agfa.

Library of Congress Cataloging-in-Publication Data

Names: Fishman, Jon M., author.
Title: Mookie Betts / Jon M. Fishman.
Description: Minneapolis : Lerner Publications, [2020] | Series: Sports all-stars | Audience: Ages: 6–12. | Audience: Grades: 4–6. | Includes bibliographical references and index.
Identifiers: LCCN 2019011844 (print) | LCCN 2019018502 (ebook) | ISBN 9781541583580 (eb pdf) | ISBN 9781541577251 (lb : alk. paper)
Subjects: LCSH: Betts, Mookie, 1992——Juvenile literature. | Baseball players—United States—Biography—Juvenile literature.
Classification: LCC GV865.B488 (ebook) | LCC GV865.B488 F57 2020 (print) | DDC 796.357 [B] —dc23

LC record available at https://lccn.loc.gov/2019011844

Manufactured in the United States of America
1-46747-47738-9/5/2019

CONTENTS

BELIEVING
IN BETTS

Mookie Betts practices batting before the 2019 All-Star Game.

Mookie Betts of the Boston Red Sox watched the baseball fly over home plate. It was a good pitch to hit, but he didn't swing. Strike one!

- **Date of birth:** October 7, 1992

- **Position:** right field

- **League:** Major League Baseball (MLB)

- **Professional Highlights:** helped Boston win the 2018 World Series; won the Gold Glove Award three years in a row; won the 2018 American League Most Valuable Player award

- **Personal Highlights:** became a father in 2018; loves to bowl and has bowled more than one perfect game; fights childhood cancer by helping to raise money to find cures

The Red Sox and the Los Angeles Dodgers were playing Game 5 of the World Series on October 28, 2018. Boston led the Dodgers 2–1 in the sixth inning when Betts stepped into the **batter's box**. The Red Sox also had the lead in the series, three games to one. They needed just one more victory to win the World Series.

The next two pitches to Betts missed the **strike zone**. Then pitch four sailed right down the middle. Betts swung, but he hit the ball **foul**.

Betts had been struggling in the World Series. He didn't have a hit in his last 13 at bats. But his teammates and fans still believed in him. During the regular season, Betts's .346 **batting average** had been the best in Major League Baseball (MLB). He also hit 32 home runs with 30 **stolen bases**.

The Red Sox won the World Series in 1918. Then more than 80 years passed without another championship. Some fans said the team was cursed. But Boston won the World Series in 2004, 2007, 2013, and 2018.

Pitch five was a little lower than pitch four. Betts bent his knees and raised his left leg. He swung the bat with incredible speed and sent the ball rocketing toward the outfield. It cleared the outfield fence for a home run!

Betts celebrates after winning the 2018 World Series.

Betts's blast gave Boston a 3–1 lead. They won the game 5–1 and took the World Series title. After the final out of the game, Betts and his teammates came together near the middle of the field. They hugged, danced, and cheered. "It's amazing," Betts said. "It's a dream come true."

A few days later, the Red Sox celebrated with their fans. The team held a parade in Boston. Fans lined the streets and cheered for their baseball heroes. Betts took it all in, filming himself and the excited crowds with his phone. He was proud to have helped bring a championship to Boston.

"RUN, RUN, RUN"

Mookie grew up in Nashville, Tennessee.

Markus "Mookie" Betts was born in Nashville, Tennessee, on October 7, 1992. Balls were his favorite toy. His mother, Diana, said Mookie always wanted a ball to play with.

Betts and his family celebrate his 2018 World Series win.

Willie Betts, Mookie's father, remembers his son speeding around the house. "He never walked," Betts said. "He would just run, run, run." Mookie loved to run and play sports.

When he was five years old, Mookie was smaller than many kids his age. That became a problem when he wanted to play Little League baseball. Some Little League coaches said he was too small to play for their teams. Mookie and some other kids couldn't find a team to play for.

Mookie's middle name is Lynn. That makes his initials MLB, just like Major League Baseball. His mother nicknamed him Mookie in honor of her sister, Cookie. His parents were also fans of the famous basketball player Mookie Blaylock.

His mother wasn't going to let her son miss out on playing baseball. She convinced a Little League official to start a new team. It would include all the players who had been left out. The new team needed a coach, so she took the job.

Mookie high fives Little League players.

By the time Mookie reached Nashville's Overton High School, he was one of the best players on his baseball team. He starred in other sports too, such as basketball and bowling. Yet it was clear to his coaches that he had a special talent for baseball. Mookie loved the sport, and his results on the field were amazing.

Mookie poses with his mom, Diana.

As a junior in 2010, he had a .549 batting average with six home runs. His record caught the attention of college **scouts**. Mookie agreed to play for the University of Tennessee after high school.

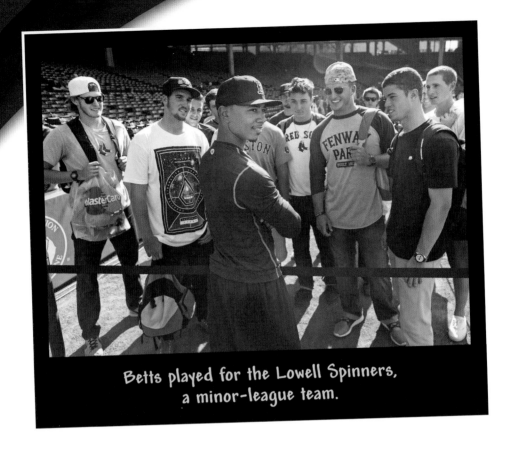

Betts played for the Lowell Spinners,
a minor-league team.

He had one more high school baseball season to play before college. He batted .509 with 29 stolen bases for Overton in 2011. In June, MLB held its annual **draft**. The Boston Red Sox chose Betts in the fifth round. He had planned to go to college after high school, but his plans changed. Betts joined the Lowell Spinners, a **minor-league team** of the Red Sox, in 2012.

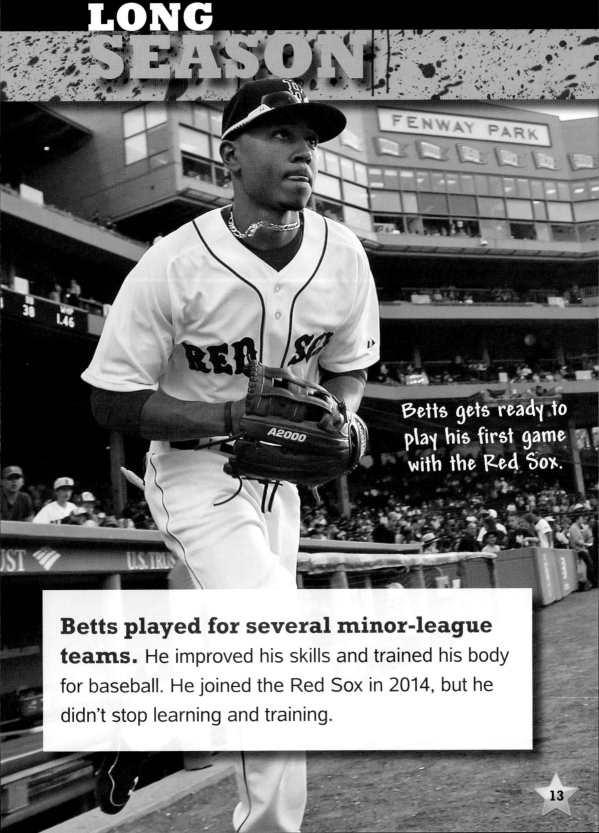

FENWAY PARK

Betts gets ready to play his first game with the Red Sox.

Betts played for several minor-league teams. He improved his skills and trained his body for baseball. He joined the Red Sox in 2014, but he didn't stop learning and training.

Betts and his teammates practice to improve their speed.

Before the start of the 2015 season, Betts went to D1 Training in Nashville. He worked on his running style and quickness at the training center. Betts said he felt more confident stealing bases after his time at D1. By the end of the 2018 season, he had stolen 110 bases in his career with the Red Sox.

Betts began lifting weights when he was in high school. He was the football team's water boy, and he lifted weights with the players during the season. He didn't play football because his mother thought it was too dangerous.

Betts continues to lift weights as a pro baseball player. During the **off-season**, he works out to build up his strength. He lifts **dumbbells** from different positions. He does pull-ups and throws heavy exercise balls. And he often does it all while wearing a weighted vest designed to make the workout more challenging.

Betts lifts dumbbells to strengthen his arms and shoulders.

The MLB regular season lasts about six months. To win the 2018 World Series, Boston played 176 regular-season and playoff games. Betts arrives at **spring training** in February each year feeling strong and ready to go. But it takes even more work to get ready to play so many games.

Betts uses a weighted vest and ball to make exercises harder.

Spring training lasts a little more than a month. Teams play games and do running, hitting, and fielding exercises. The workouts are designed to prepare players for the long season rather than improve their

Betts doesn't like to feel full during games. He eats a light snack before taking the field. His go-to pregame foods are fruit, a smoothie, or a peanut butter and jelly sandwich.

skills. "We know how to play the game of baseball but you have to get your body ready for it," Betts said.

Betts practices throwing during spring training.

CLOTHING, BOWLING,
AND KIDS

Betts and his family react to him being named the 2018 Most Valuable Player.

Betts spends time with his daughter, Kynlee, before receiving awards for the 2018 season.

Winning the 2018 World Series on October 28 was a huge thrill for Betts. Nine days later, something even more exciting happened. Betts and his partner, Brianna, became parents of a baby girl. He said it was a day he would always remember.

Betts gives back to the community by working with children's groups. One Mission fights childhood cancer. Pitching in for Kids fights bullying and teaches teamwork skills to kids in the New England area. Betts helps raise money for both groups with bowling tournaments and other fun events.

Betts takes to the radio airwaves to encourage listeners to donate to cancer patients and their families.

Betts has become Boston's most valuable player. He was a huge part of the team's success in 2018, and he's one of the game's most popular athletes. That's why he decided to step up his fashion game.

If Mookie Betts wasn't a superstar baseball player, he might be a famous bowler. Betts's mother loves to bowl, and she taught her son the sport when he was three years old. He's been bowling ever since.

In 2017, Betts competed in the **World Series of Bowling**. In one round, he rolled a perfect-game score of 300. He's

bowled several perfect games in his career. Betts is the only member of the **Professional Bowlers Association** who has won the **MLB World Series**.

Betts bowling during a tournament hosted by National Basketball Association star Chris Paul

Betts said he used to wear sweatpants to the ballpark. His friends convinced him that as a famous athlete, he should always look good. You never know when a fan might snap a photo for social media. Betts likes a wide variety of outfits and styles. "Your look one day can be totally different than the next day, and for me, it's all about owning that," he said.

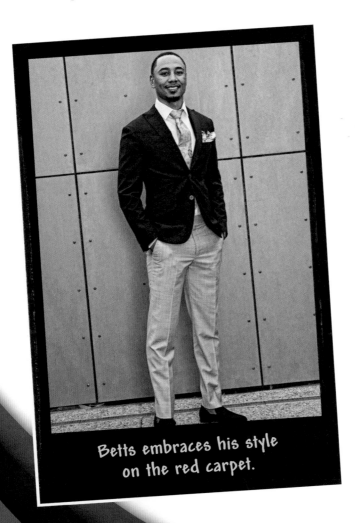

Betts embraces his style on the red carpet.

Betts (second from the right) and some of his teammates have fun during the 2019 Red Sox Winter Weekend.

The Red Sox had fun with fashion in 2018. Betts and his teammates sometimes wore group outfits as they traveled for games. They wore red, white, and blue clothes to match the US flag on Independence Day. They wore tracksuits, beach clothing, and other fun outfits that year.

Betts catches a fly ball.

In high school, Betts played second base, shortstop, and center field.
As a minor-league player, he spent most of his time at second base. He was ready to play for the Red Sox by 2014.

Dustin Pedroia won the American League Most Valuable Player award in 2008.

But there was a problem. The Red Sox already had Dustin Pedroia, a superstar second baseman.

If Betts wanted to play for the Red Sox, he needed a new position. He began playing games as a right fielder. Even though he spent time in the outfield in high school, it wasn't an easy switch at such an advanced level of baseball. "It was tough at first," he said. "I didn't realize outfield was that tough."

Betts figured it out fast. He won American League (AL) Gold Glove Awards in 2016, 2017, and 2018. That meant he was voted the best right fielder in the AL for those seasons.

Winning the Gold Glove in 2018 for the third time was one of many big events in a huge year for Betts. He won his first World Series and became a father. He also won the AL Most Valuable Player (MVP) award.

Betts holding his 2017 Gold Glove award

Betts hitting a home run

After the 2020 season, Betts's contract will end. He'll be free to join any team he chooses. The Red Sox want to keep their superstar outfielder, and the feeling seems to be mutual. "I love it here in Boston," Betts said.

All-Star Stats

It's hard to blast a home run in professional baseball. Hitting the ball just right takes a lot of practice at any level. When pitchers throw the ball nearly 100 miles (160 km) per hour as they do in MLB, the task becomes even more difficult. No Boston player has ever hit four home runs in a game. But Betts has hit three in a game more than once. Look at where he ranks on Boston's all-time list of three-home-run games.

Red Sox Player Career Three-Home-Run Games

Mookie Betts	**4**
Ted Williams	3
Nomar Garciaparra	2
Jim Rice	2
Mo Vaughn	2

Source Notes

7 Nicole Yang, "What the Red Sox Had to Say after Winning the 2018 World Series," Boston.com, October 29, 2018, https://www.boston.com/sports/boston-red -sox/2018/10/29/red-sox-world-series-quotes.

9 Jen McCaffrey, "The Story of Mookie Betts' Rise from Nashville to Boston Red Sox Franchise Cornerstone," MassLive, July 15, 2015, https://www.masslive.com/ redsox/index.ssf/2015/07/boston_red_sox_mookie_betts .html.

17 Sean Penney, "Red Sox Outfielder Mookie Betts Discusses Spring Workout Routine Fueled by BODYARMOR," FanSided, accessed March 3, 2019, https://bosoxinjection .com/2018/03/26/red-sox-outfielder-mookie-betts -discusses-spring-workout-routine-fueled-bodyarmor/.

22 Ben Pardee, "Mookie Betts Wants You to Know That Baseball Players Can Be Stylish, Too," GQ, July 16, 2018, https://www.gq.com/story/mookie-betts-red-sox-all-star -game-interview.

25 Adam London, "Mookie Betts Sheds Light on Transition from Second Baseman to Outfielder," NESN, July 16, 2018, https://nesn.com/2018/07/mookie-betts-sheds-light -on-transition-from-second-baseman-to-outfielder/.

27 Chad Finn, "When Will We Know What It Is Mookie Betts Wants?," Boston.com, March 20, 2019, https://www .boston.com/sports/boston-red-sox/2019/03/20/mookie -betts-contract.

Glossary

batter's box: the area near home plate where the batter stands

batting average: the ratio of a batter's hits per times at bat

draft: an event in which teams take turns choosing new players

dumbbells: bars with weighted ends used for exercise

foul: outside the field of play

minor-league team: a baseball team on which players train and hope to move up to Major League Baseball

off-season: the time of year when a sports league is inactive

scouts: people who judge the talent of baseball players

spring training: a series of workouts and games for players to get ready for the MLB season

stolen bases: when base runners advance to a base they aren't entitled to, usually as the pitcher throws the ball to home plate

strike zone: the area above home plate that a pitched ball must pass through to be a strike

Bates, Greg. *Mookie Betts*. Lake Elmo, MN: Focus Readers, 2019.

Lajiness, Katie. *Boston Red Sox*. Minneapolis: Big Buddy Books, 2019.

MLB
https://www.mlb.com/

Official Site of the Boston Red Sox
https://www.mlb.com/redsox

Professional Bowlers Association
https://www.pba.com/

Savage, Jeff. *Baseball Super Stats*. Minneapolis: Lerner Publications, 2018.

Index

Photo Acknowledgments

Image credits: Billie Weiss/Boston Red Sox/Getty Images, pp. 4, 7, 10, 14, 15, 16, 18, 19, 20, 23, 26; Davel5957/Getty Images, p. 8; Rob Leiter/MLB Photos/Getty Images, p. 9; Rodin Eckenroth/FilmMagic/Getty Images, p. 11; Jim Davis/The Boston Globe/Getty Images, pp. 12, 13; Christopher Evans/MediaNews Group/Boston Herald/Getty Images, p. 17; Bob Levey/Getty Images, pp. 21, 24; Joey Terrill/MLB Photos/Getty Images, p. 22; Brace Hemmelgarn/Minnesota Twins/Getty Images, p. 25; Sean M. Haffey/Getty Images, p. 27.

Cover Image: Omar Rawlings/Getty Images.